Easy-To-Say
First Words
A Focus on Final Consonants

Developed by a
Speech-Language Pathologist

Cara Tambellini Danielson M.A. CCC-SLP

Illustrated by Mary Tambellini

ISBN: 1494284022
ISBN-13: 9781494284022

About this book:

This book, designed for both speech-language pathologists and parents, exposes the child repeatedly to final consonants in everyday words. Early in speech development, many children struggle to produce final consonants. For example, they may say "ee" instead of "eat", "bo" instead of "boat", or "uh" instead of "up." When this occurs, their parents often misunderstand their attempts to communicate.

The target words in this book are easy-to-say because they are one-syllable words that contain early-developing consonants (for example: p,b,m,t,d,k,g,h). Since the target words are common first words, this book can be read with any child who is learning to talk.

There are three categories of final sounds included in the book: words that end with /p/, words that end with /t/, and words that end with /k/. You can read them all together or read one section at a time, depending on the child's interest.

Guide for reading this book:

1. Make sure your child can **see your face** and the book while you are reading so that he can see the way your mouth forms the words.

2. After your child becomes familiar with the book, **pause before the last word on each page** to see if she will "fill in the blank." For example, "Hop hop hop. The baby bunnies...(pause)." As your child uses more and more words, she may be able to say the last sentence for herself as well as label other items on the page.

3. **Use gestures** when reading the book and **encourage play** when possible. For instance, you can:
   - *Kick a ball* after you read the sentence, "Roll the ball and kick."
   - *Point up in the air* when you say, "The hot air balloon goes up."
   - *Hold a toy truck and pretend to make it beep* when you read, "beep beep beep."
   - *Pretend to drink from an empty cup* when you read, "Drink from the cup."
   - *Touch the sun and say, "ouch, hot!"* after you read, "The sun is hot."
   - *Hop together* after you read, "hop hop hop."
   - *Pretend to blow out the candles or take a bite of the cake* when you read, "Eat the cake."

4. **Respond with enthusiasm** to any attempt your child makes at saying a word (even if it does not resemble the actual word). If he mispronounces a word, you can repeat the word or phrase correctly after he says it. For example, if he says "bee bee" while pointing to a truck, respond by saying, "**Beep beep**, the truck **beeps!**" You can emphasize the mispronounced word so that he can hear the correct pronunciation, but do not insist that he repeat the correct pronunciation.

5. **Make book reading fun**. Let your child lead when you read together. Spend more time on pages in which your child shows interest. Label and talk about other items on the page as your child points. Don't insist that the book is read from cover to cover. Instead, stop reading when your child shows signs that she is ready for another activity.

Up

Up

Up

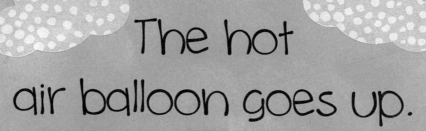

The hot
air balloon goes up.

Mop

Mop Mop

Mop

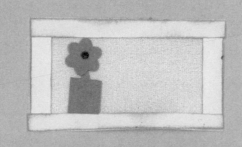

Clean with
a mop.

Hop

Hop

Hop

The baby
bunnies hop.

Beep

Beep

Beep

The truck says beep.

Cup

Cup

Cup

Drink from the cup.

Hat

Hat

Hat

The owl
wears a
hat.

Bat

Bat

Bat

Fly away black bat.

Hot

Hot

Hot

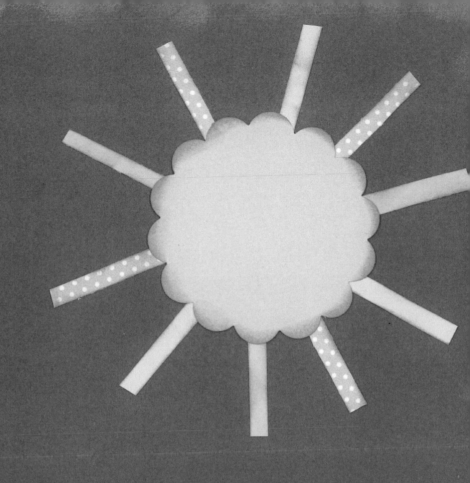

The sun is hot.

Eat

Eat

Eat

Two hungry
mice eat.

Boat
Boat

Boat

Sail in the boat.

Book

Book

Book

Read a book.

Kick

Kick

Kick

Roll the ball
and kick.

Cake
Cake
Cake

Eat the
birthday cake.

Bike Bike Bike

Ride a red bike.

Duck

Duck

Duck

There is a
swimming duck.

About the Author:

Cara Tambellini Danielson is a California licensed Speech-Language Pathologist. She holds a Certification of Clinical Competence from the American Speech-Language and Hearing Association (ASHA). She received her B.A. in Psychology from Northwestern University and her M.A. in Communication Sciences and Disorders from Northwestern University. Cara specializes in pediatric speech and language development. She has experience working in a variety of settings, including private practice, early intervention, schools, and rehabilitation hospitals. She currently lives in Santa Monica, California.

About the Illustrator:

Mary Tambellini is a card designer for her Pittsburgh-based business, A Mary Card and More, where she designs greeting cards and invitations. She hopes her artwork makes children smile.

Made in the USA
Middletown, DE
03 October 2017